S0-AYZ-595

He gathers your tears

He gathers your tears

Words of Comfort for a Widow's Heart

Phylis Moore

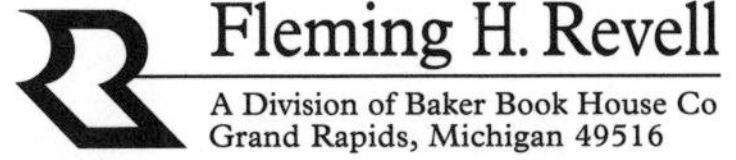
Fleming H. Revell
A Division of Baker Book House Co
Grand Rapids, Michigan 49516

Published by Fleming H. Revell
a division of Baker Book House Company
P.O. Box 6287, Grand Rapids, MI 49516-6287

Printed in the United States of America

ISBN 0-8007-1784-8

Library of Congress Cataloging-in-Publication Data is on file at the Library of Congress, Washington, D.C.

For current information about all releases from Baker Book House, visit our web site:

http://www.bakerbooks.com

In memory of
Roger Allan Moore
gentle, gracious, godly, a bit goofy
my love and my friend
Psalm 34:3

For our children
Bonnie and Coleen
and Floyd, Clara, and Trudy
each of whom never wavered in support
of me while they themselves
mourned deeply for
their father, son, and brother

Introduction

The day of my husband's memorial service felt like a party. Friends came to my home and fussed over me and my two daughters. They ironed our clothes and painted our fingernails. Just before leaving the house for the service, a group of us gathered around my bed and prayed. The church was packed with friends, and I wore a red dress. I was oddly radiant. I greeted hundreds of people afterward at the dessert reception. You'd have thought it was New Year's Eve.

Then I crashed. For the next few weeks, I could hardly turn around in my own kitchen. I ached all over. I could not sleep. I cried and cried and was totally confused. Acute emotional pain surged through my whole body, which felt as if it had been sawn in two and the raw edges set on fire. The shock of Roger's death was fading, and reality was taking its place.

Shock is the first phase of grief; it enables us to endure a tragic loss and go through the necessary motions of living. I call this "emotional

anesthesia," which was my condition at my husband's service. When the "anesthesia" wears off, however, pain sweeps through and burns hot. The process of grieving then begins in earnest.

People have varied reactions to bereavement, for none of our circumstances or temperaments are exactly the same. I think I am one who "took it" the hardest and grieved "the longest," so now I feel I can relate to just about anyone's grief experience. I have found that you don't get *over* grief, you have to go *through* it. You have to realize that there is no standard time frame for the end of grief. Grieving and grief work are *tasks to be accomplished* at your own pace.

Part of grief recovery for many people is putting their feelings on paper, which is exactly what I did. As I wrote and read my Bible, I noticed that God had a response for each issue I confronted as I tried to adjust to confusing and frightening new realities. I wished I had my favorite verses in one small volume that I could carry around with me. I conceived this book for that purpose. Stash it in your purse; stick it in a pocket; hug it to your heart.

When the "party" is over for you and you feel as if you've been rocketed into outer space, may you find that *He Gathers Your Tears* normalizes your experiences and validates your emotions.

I aim to assure you that you are not going crazy and to offer the hope that all will be well in time. God understands your turmoil and your worrisome feelings. He does not scold you for them, he addresses them with the loving intention to help you through this hard time. I call his words "love letters," because he has pledged to be our husband now, and his promises are in writing.

Your Maker is your husband—The LORD Almighty is his name.

Isaiah 54:5a

I wrote . . .

This phrase repeats and repeats in my head, flooding me with comfort and a joy that makes me weep. The result is the strength to go on.

He wrote . . .

. . . loved by God the Father and kept by Jesus Christ.

Jude 1b

I wrote . . .

Why did he have to die? Why am I a "surviving spouse"? Wasn't it a mistake to take him? I can't see any reason why you didn't take me instead. He was the one who had all the knowledge and wisdom and skill in counseling.

He was the good one. Even two days before he died, he insisted I go to our bed to sleep, even though he had to sit up in the recliner all night. He said, "Don't worry about me tonight; leave me in the Lord's hands. It's a safe place to be."

He wrote . . .

The righteous perish,
  and no one ponders it in his heart;
devout men are taken away,
  and no one understands
that the righteous are taken away
  to be spared from evil.
Those who walk uprightly
  enter into peace;
  they find rest as they lie in death.

Isaiah 57:1–2

I wrote . . .

I am Jacob: "*She* struggles with God." Has he ever failed me? I want to shout, "Yes!" I can't get the comfort I used to from the Word. I feel as if God let me down. I clung so hard to verses of hope, and my hopes were smashed. I staked our future and Roger's life on a promise that God would lead us in the best way for us. Now the verse only stabs and confuses me. I know God does not lie, but this seems to be wrong, a mockery of my faith.

But of course, I interpreted "what is best for you" as being Roger's healing. I have to trust that his last days *were* the "best" for him as he spent them at home surrounded by the love and comfort of family and friends.

He wrote . . .

This is what the LORD says—
your Redeemer, the Holy One of Israel:
"I am the LORD your God,
who teaches you what is best for you,
who directs you in the way you should
go."

Isaiah 48:17

"Your name will no longer be Jacob, but Israel, because you have struggled with God . . . and have overcome."

Genesis 32:28

I wrote . . .

Where is he? It just does not seem possible that he's not here anymore. I miss you, dear one. I want to touch your face, to trace the O'Neill smile on your lips. Lord, would you please tell him "Hi" and that I still love him?

He wrote . . .

We are confident, I say, and would prefer to be away from the body and at home with the Lord.

2 Corinthians 5:8

I wrote . . .

I cried and screamed and got really mad—mad at God and mad at Roger for not being here. Mercy, mercy. I had to "smother" myself with a verse in order to be able to bear the misery and depression. I drew "feathers" over me and repeated the verse until I fell asleep.

He wrote . . .

Have mercy on me, O God, have mercy
on me,
for in you my soul takes refuge.
I will take refuge in the shadow of your
wings
until the disaster has passed.

Psalm 57:1

I wrote . . .

I desperately need to talk to someone. I grab the phone, make call after call, and find no one at home. Please, God, please. I *have* to talk to someone or I'll go crazy.

He wrote . . .

Trust in him at all times, O people;
pour out your hearts to him,
for God is our refuge.

Psalm 62:8

I wrote . . .

O Lord, I just feel like crawling into a hole (my bed will do) and curling up into a ball. If only I could fade away and be done with this fear, uncertainty, loneliness, and pain.

He wrote . . .

He hides me away under his roof
on the day of evil,
he folds me in the recesses of his tent,
sets me high on a rock.

Now my head is held high
above the enemies who surround
me;
in his tent I will offer
sacrifices of acclaim.

Psalm 27:5–6 NJB

I wrote . . .

Roger did trust you with his life and for the end result of his illness. But I've agonized over the question, "Did he die before his time?" Was it shortsighted not to continue medical treatment? Was he going to die on that certain day regardless of the path we chose?

He wrote . . .

Man's days are determined;
  you have decreed the number of his
    months
  and have set limits he cannot exceed.

Job 14:5

I wrote . . .

I cried all the way home, then sat in the car and started to wail. I never knew I could make such sounds. Feeling abandoned, I rolled down the window and searched the sky, pleading, "Where are you, God? Don't you see me? Don't you know my agony? You promised to help me. Where are you?"

He wrote . . .

O Lord, be not far off;
 O my Strength, come quickly to help
  me. . . .
He has not despised or disdained
 the suffering of the afflicted one;
he has not hidden his face from him
 but has listened to his cry for help.

Psalm 22:19, 24

I wrote . . .

It's after twelve now, and I wish I could stay up forever in this melancholy midnight until I die of being awake.

He wrote . . .

God is within her, she will not fall;
God will help her at break of day.

Psalm 46:5

I wrote . . .

I'm just hanging on by my toenails—praising and singing without feeling, in the face of my senseless life.

He wrote . . .

Though the fig tree does not bud
   and there are no grapes on the vines,
   though the olive crop fails
   and the fields produce no food,
though there are no sheep in the pen
   and no cattle in the stalls,
yet I will rejoice in the Lord,
   I will be joyful in God my Savior.
The Sovereign Lord is my strength;
   he makes my feet like the feet of a
      deer,
   he enables me to go on the heights.

Habakkuk 3:17–19

I wrote . . .

I don't understand all this pain and emptiness. I need hope, but all I get is sand. Will my life have any meaning without him?

He wrote . . .

"I am now going to allure her;
I will lead her into the desert
and speak tenderly to her.
There I will give her back her vineyards,
and will make the Valley of [Trouble] a
door of hope."

Hosea 2:14–15

I wrote . . .

I think my brain melted. I can barely deal with day-to-day finances. I haven't balanced my checkbook in months. I forgot to record a cash withdrawal, which cost me three times as much in overdraft charges. On top of it all, in the middle of the night I remembered a statement that I had crammed in the cupboard. What was it for? Car insurance? It turned out to be my property tax bill. God had reminded me, and I paid it just in time!

He wrote . . .

Yahweh is merciful and upright, our God is tenderness. Yahweh looks after the simple, when I was brought low he gave me strength.

Psalm 116:5–6 NJB

I wrote . . .

Depression has moved in (I hope not to stay, but it feels like it). I feel like a baby who needs twenty-four-hour care. I just want to hide under my covers and sleep forever. The thought of having to keep cooking and grocery shopping and planning meals is overwhelming. How does anyone survive this? I don't think I can go on. I don't want to.

He wrote . . .

"I have loved you with an everlasting
love;
I have drawn you with loving-
kindness.
I will build you up again
and you will be rebuilt."

Jeremiah 31:3–4

I wrote . . .

Flannel sheets and feather pillows absorb tears quite well.

He wrote . . .

I am worn out from groaning;
all night long I flood my bed with weeping
and drench my couch with tears.

Psalm 6:6

I wrote . . .

I suffered a "quicksand" evening tonight. I felt like I was going down for the third time, then at the last minute, God reached down, grabbed me by the hair so to speak, and pulled me up. The rescue came in simple ways—an encouraging telephone call from out of town, a favorite video, and the unexpected visit from a friend who had a gift for me—a cozy red nightgown!

He wrote . . .

When you pass through the waters,
  I will be with you;
and when you pass through the
    rivers,
  they will not sweep over you.
When you walk through the fire,
  you will not be burned;
the flames will not set you ablaze.

Isaiah 43:2

I wrote . . .

I have a confession. Sometimes I get so desperate to talk to a man that I go to a car lot and pretend I am looking for a car. Well, I *am* looking for a car. It's just that I can't *buy* one right now. How pathetic. How embarrassing. I miss talking to a man. I miss hearing a man's voice. I miss intelligent communication with the male perspective. At least at the car lot, I get *some* conversation and male attention, even if it is from some anonymous car salesman.

He wrote . . .

"Call to me and I will answer you and tell you great and unsearchable things you do not know."

Jeremiah 33:3

I wrote . . .

I drove to an isolated spot in the parking lot and just bawled and bawled.

He wrote . . .

My intercessor is my friend as my eyes pour out tears to God.

Job 16:20

I wrote . . .

I cannot bear to wake up and face another day. I need courage every morning just to get up. The only way I can put my feet on the floor is to reach first for the little card that I keep by my bed and read it again.

He wrote . . .

Yet this I call to mind
   and therefore I have hope:
Because of the LORD's great love we are
      not
      consumed,
   for his compassions never fail.
They are new every morning;
   great is your faithfulness.

Lamentations 3:21–23

I wrote . . .

I feel like I've gone back three months, and the grief is fresh all over again. C. S. Lewis was right in saying that grief feels like fear. I went to sleep crying and I'm awaking crying, mainly because I'm scared and more lonely than ever. I just had a bad dream, and fear was a big part of it. The fear and the loneliness seem unbearable.

He wrote . . .

When I am afraid,
  I will trust in you.
In God, whose word I praise,
  in God I trust; I will not be afraid.
  What can mortal man do to me?

Psalm 56:3–4

I wrote . . .

How many times have I gotten into the shower and leaned against the wall, hot water pounding my body, wondering how I could go on? The physical sensation is the only break I have from despair and uncertainty. I stand for a long time because I don't know what to do once I open the door and step out.

He wrote . . .

The steps of a good man are ordered by the LORD, and he [delights] in his way.

Psalm 37:23 KJV

I wrote . . .

I am worn out trying to do everything right. I must not be so hard on myself. I need to lose the "shoulds." I can only do what I can do.

He wrote . . .

As a father has compassion on his
children,
so the LORD has compassion on those
who fear him;
for he knows how we are formed,
he remembers that we are dust.

Psalm 103:13–14

I wrote . . .

I think I am going crazy. What will people think? I worry about money. I worry about the kids. I worry about my future. My imagination is spinning out of control.

He wrote . . .

Thou will keep him in perfect peace, whose mind [imagination] is stayed on thee.

Isaiah 26:3 KJV

I wrote . . .

Yes, yes, yes—my dreams are dead. All I had, was, and hoped for is gone. I'm mad, and that makes me stubborn. I will *not* give up, because I *know* God is wise and merciful. He made this promise, and I'm holding him to it until it is fulfilled and I get to go "back"!

He wrote . . .

"I will gather you from all the . . . places where I have banished you," declares the LORD, "and will bring you back to the place from which I carried you into exile."

Jeremiah 29:14

I wrote . . .

All this confusion and panic is certainly not from God. In spite of my multiplied losses—friends, income, social life, partnership in ministry, identity, purpose, confidence—*I will trust.*

He wrote . . .

Though he slay me, yet will I trust in him.

Job 13:15a KJV

I wrote . . .

Am I "stuck" in this grief process? I heard a counselor say that some people do stay "stuck" because "the intimacy of pain is better than no intimacy at all." Is that what's going on? If I "get over" this pain, will I "get over" Roger, losing all connection with him? Will I lose all intimacy in my life? Can intimacy with God take its place?

He wrote . . .

Whom have I in heaven but you?
  And earth has nothing I desire besides
    you.
My flesh and my heart may fail,
  but God is the strength of my heart
  and my portion forever.

Psalm 73:25–26

I wrote . . .

Lord, I'm such a nurturer. I was *meant* to be this way. You *made* me this way. I'm a "helpmate" with no mate to help. Ever since I can remember, I wanted to be a wife and mommy. I find it so *natural* to reach out to a man, to soothe, to support, to encourage, to help replace a burden with a smile. How do I stifle that now? Stifle what I was created to be? To do?

He wrote . . .

An unmarried woman is concerned about the Lord's affairs. Her aim is to be devoted to the Lord in both body and spirit. . . . I am saying this for your own good, not to restrict you, but that you may live in a right way in undivided devotion to the Lord.

1 Corinthians 7:34–35

I wrote . . .

I'm so glad she said, "You do what you have to do to get through the day." That meant crying again today for no apparent reason. I've been trying to justify or excuse it to myself. No . . . I just had to.

He wrote . . .

Jesus wept.

John 11:35

I wrote . . .

The last week or so, I feel like I've started a new round of battle—like I've been through a war of hurt and suffering. I went to the hospice office on Tuesday and talked to the grief counselor for the first time. I'm going to do that for a while until I get all the help I can there. I'm just kinda numb again with all the pain and emptiness.

The counselor told me that the five-month mark—where I am right now—is harder than the first couple of months after a death. I was beginning to feel in the last month or so that I was making wonderful progress and should be starting to get things together. I was kind of stuffing my hurt and ignoring it, which didn't work for long. It's still here, and I still have to go through it. Right now I feel like a prisoner who just has to sit still and keep absorbing the blows and the slaps.

He wrote . . .

"Do not be afraid or discouraged because of this vast army. For the battle is not yours, but God's. . . . You will not have to fight this battle. Take up your positions; stand firm and see the deliverance the LORD will give you."

2 Chronicles 20:15b, 17

I wrote . . .

Another lonely Friday drags into the middle of the night. I can't bring myself to turn off the light, although I am very tired. I guess I'm trying to delay the start of tomorrow. I'll probably have to cry a little first.

He wrote . . .

Thou countest up my sleepless hours,
my tears are gathered in thy bottle—
are they not noted in thy book?

Psalm 56:8 MOFFATT

I wrote . . .

Lucy was carrying on today, crying, because her sixteen-year-old son is away for the summer, and she misses him. I wanted to demand, "What about me? You want to know missing? Try a dead husband!" I'm not proud of this. I'm sorry I could not feel more compassion for her. Perhaps I did exhibit love though, because I held my tongue and listened to her, silently absorbing the invisible pain.

He wrote . . .

It is commendable if a man bears up under the pain of unjust suffering because he is conscious of God.

1 Peter 2:19

I wrote . . .

I stopped to think how tough I have to be now; how I'm forced to do for myself. Then I remember what it feels like to have a husband who cares about me, and I cry. It would be so wonderful to have a man to collapse on. He would take the worries and emotional weight for a while. It gets tiring being "tough." He'd be concerned and help with my problems. Protecting me would be his joy. He would treat me with consideration and honor my weaknesses. He would understand that I am his partner in spiritual life and blessings. His attitudes toward me would be sweet and generous, as Roger's were.

Come to think of it, the ideal husband I just described sounds exactly like God! Who could improve on him?

He wrote . . .

For your Maker is your husband—
  the Lord Almighty is his name—
the Holy One of Israel is your
    Redeemer;
  he is called the God of all the earth.

Isaiah 54:5

I wrote . . .

Lord, so much of what I've written is sad. I want you to catch me being thankful more and more. I must not let self-pity in. I have so much.

He wrote . . .

The Lord is my strength and my shield;
my heart trusts in him, and I am helped.
My heart leaps for joy
and I will give thanks to him in song.

Psalm 28:7

I wrote . . .

Selling Roger's car has been a hassle, adding to the emotional anxiety of parting with it. I tried advertising it in the newspaper and leaving it at a friend's gas station. When those things didn't work, I put it on consignment at a small car lot nearby. The owner, good old "Jack," turned out to be a crook. I happened to check on the car one day and found that the stereo was gone.

"Burglars," Jack said.

"Oh? When were you going to inform me?" I asked.

"Well, I was just going to replace it."

Not believing his fishy story, I took the car back and finally sold it myself.

He wrote . . .

"I will come near to you for judgment. I will be quick to testify against . . . those . . . who oppress the widows and the fatherless, . . ." says the LORD Almighty.

Malachi 3:5

I wrote . . .

Roger never called me "Honey," but he used to call me other affectionate nicknames. I miss hearing him say, "Sweetheart," "Beautiful," "Sweet Love," "Babe," "Phylis J."

He wrote . . .

"Fear not, for I have redeemed you;
  I have summoned you by name;
    you are mine."

Isaiah 43:1b

I wrote . . .

Here I am again, at midnight, trying to figure out my life. Certain goals won't go away, and yet I don't have the energy to pursue them. Lord, you will have to tell me. I don't want to waste my life wondering. I need an outlet for my love and creativity and really desire to accomplish things for you.

He wrote . . .

But as for me, I watch in hope for the
    Lord,
  I wait for God my Savior;
  my God will hear me.

Micah 7:7

I wrote . . .

How much longer can I stand this feeling of aloneness? I am sitting here alone, listening to a speaker with a marvelous mind. He makes us laugh, and he loves your Word passionately. I connect deeply to what he's saying. I long to share this spiritual experience with someone—a soul mate—in tune with me and what we're hearing. Being without that person, I feel isolated, desolate, unloved, and unknown. That is what is so painful—being unknown.

He wrote . . .

O Lord, you have searched me
 and you know me.
You know when I sit and when I rise;
 you perceive my thoughts from
  afar.

Psalm 139:1–2

I wrote . . .

I have learned to have no guilt over spending most of a day napping! I usually feel like I have to be doing something all the time. Someone told me, "taking care of your body is productive." What a freeing thought! Grieving is hard work that takes its toll on the body as well as the emotions, and we need to allow for that.

So now when I need it, I take an "Elijah Day." When Elijah was exhausted and depressed, God's solution was sleep and eat, sleep and eat! I took a nap one afternoon for two and a half hours; I didn't realize I was that tired. Often my bluest days have been relieved by permitting myself to enjoy an "Elijah Day."

He wrote . . .

Elijah was afraid and ran for his life. . . . He came to a broom tree, sat down under it and prayed that he might die. . . . Then he lay down under the tree and fell asleep. All at once an angel touched him and said, "Get up and eat." . . . He ate and drank and then lay down again. The angel of the LORD came back a second time and touched him and said, "Get up and eat, for the journey is too much for you." So he got up and ate and drank [and was] strengthened by that food.

1 Kings 19:3–8a

I wrote . . .

I had the poignant privilege of visiting a newly bereaved family today. The widow is very young. Not much older than twenty. Help me, O Lord, to pass on the comfort I've received. I certainly can cry with them. My pain is not in vain, but what a solemn, heart-wrenching assignment you've given me.

He wrote . . .

Praise be to the God and father of our Lord Jesus Christ, the Father of compassion and the God of all comfort, who comforts us in all our troubles, so that we can comfort those in any trouble with the comfort we ourselves have received from God.

2 Corinthians 1:3–4

I wrote . . .

I can't fathom living the rest of my life without sex. This wonderful gift to a marriage is off-limits for me now. I try not to think of a hundred things that have to do with love, romance, my femininity, tenderness, men. I try not to think of them so that I can keep my thoughts pure. I guess I have to pray for the "gift of celibacy" and be grateful that there are more important things to live for. This is truly another way to suffer.

He wrote . . .

Therefore, since Christ suffered in his body, arm yourselves also with the same attitude because he who has suffered in his body is done with sin. As a result, he does not live the rest of his earthly life for evil human desires, but rather for the will of God.

1 Peter 4:1–2

I wrote . . .

I went out to buy some pansies, but I wondered if I should spend the money. Sometimes I even hesitate to buy a magazine. I often just decide I'd better not.

He wrote . . .

The Lord tears down the proud man's
house
but he keeps the widow's boundaries
intact.

Proverbs 15:25

I wrote . . .

My heart is so heavy that I struggle to trust the Lord and get through every hour. It takes sheer grit to make the choice to praise him. I sure don't feel like it, and I certainly don't see any relief in all this.

He wrote . . .

"He who sacrifices thank offerings honors
me,
and he prepares the way
so that I may show him the salvation of
God."

Psalm 50:23

I wrote . . .

Betty told me she and her husband often rode motorcycles together. After his death, riding gave her a way to cope with loneliness and enjoy intimate fellowship with God. One day she was riding alone through the Rockies. A summer storm descended, blowing and soaking her, reducing visibility to four or five feet. She dared not look down at the controls. Suddenly, two red lights, each about seven inches across, appeared in front of her, guiding her through the downpour. Only later did she have time to wonder if they were on the back of a truck.

Finally visibility increased as the sky lightened. For a fraction of a second she glanced down at the control panel, and looking up again saw that the lights were gone. What she did see was the mountain rising straight up on her left and a sheer drop down the mountainside on her right. No other traffic was in sight. She firmly believes an angelic escort led her safely through the pass!

He wrote . . .

For he will command his angels concerning you
to guard you in all your ways.

Psalm 91:11

I wrote . . .

I just feel numb and drab—not intensely lonely or intensely anything. Hope dims, and I am weary. Well, ha! I know which verse to "take" for that!

He wrote . . .

And let us not be weary in well doing: for in due season we shall reap, if we faint not.

Galatians 6:9 KJV

I wrote . . .

Marshmallows are on a low shelf at the grocery store (kids' eye level, I guess). Today as I bent down to pick up a bag, memories flooded me—Roger used to raid the marshmallows I had put away for a special recipe—and I burst into tears. I fervently hoped no one saw me crying. Ambushed. It happened again when I saw a store mannequin dressed like Roger used to dress. I had to run to a wall and pretend to be interested in napkin rings so no one would see my tears. Ambushed. Surprised by a fresh wave of grief. Anytime, anywhere. Unexpected. Slashes my heart.

He wrote . . .

"The Lord your God is with you,
he is mighty to save.
He will take great delight in you,
he will quiet you with his love,
he will rejoice over you with
singing."

Zephaniah 3:17

I wrote . . .

After eleven months, I'm still wearing my wedding rings because I still feel married. But all of a sudden, I look at them and feel like a hypocrite. How can I wear wedding rings when I'm not married anymore? I'm not a wife. Who am I? A widow. *Widow* is such an ugly word. Me? Now?

He wrote . . .

"Do not be afraid; you will not suffer
shame.
Do not fear disgrace; you will not be
humiliated.
You will . . . remember no more the
reproach of your widowhood."

Isaiah 54:4

I wrote . . .

I can't sleep, I can't sleep, I can't sleep. I'm sitting here with another headache. A friend just called and invited me to lunch tomorrow, but I'm such a mess. I don't know what I'd talk about. I feel like I have no personality. I feel weak; I am weak; I'm supposed to delight when I'm weak. This is a test. I want to pass this time.

I grit my teeth and say, without an ounce of feeling, "I will delight, I will delight. . . ."

O God, I feel rotten; money is a problem; I don't know what to do. Thank you that you have a plan, though I don't have a clue.

He wrote . . .

I delight in weaknesses, in insults, in hardships, in persecutions, in difficulties. For when I am weak, then I am strong.

2 Corinthians 12:10

I wrote . . .

I heard of a young boy named Max, who was filled with rage over his father's death. He blamed his mother and left hate notes in her purse. He set his mattress on fire. The last time he yelled "I hate you" at her, God impressed on her to yell back, "Well, I love you more than you hate me!" Max ran into her arms, crying, and his healing began.

He wrote . . .

"All your sons will be taught by the
LORD,
and great will be your children's
peace."

Isaiah 54:13

I wrote . . .

I simply cannot read the Song of Songs anymore. It is just too romantic. Oh, I know it has spiritual application and all that, but I have taught marriage classes on intimacy from this book! Is there any verse here for a single woman? Wow, maybe at the end of chapter eight. Since God is now my husband, I can apply this verse to my relationship with him and make it my aim.

He wrote . . .

I have become in his eyes like one bringing contentment.

Song of Songs 8:10b

I wrote . . .

I am amazed at the strength God has given me today on only four or five hours of sleep. I claimed the promise that the strength I needed would equal the day's demands. When he says that "the bolts of your gates will be iron and bronze," I take that as a promise that I will not fall apart!

He wrote . . .

"The bolts of your gates will be iron and
bronze,
and your strength will equal your
days."

Deuteronomy 33:25

I wrote . . .

My friend Kathie was widowed in her early twenties when her husband died in a boating accident. Left with two children in diapers, she figuratively ripped open her chest, held her heart in her hands, and pleaded, "Okay, God, you see all this pain. What are you going to do with it?"

He wrote . . .

You, O God, do see trouble and grief;
you consider it to take it in hand.
The victim commits [herself] to you;
you are the helper of the fatherless.

Psalm 10:14

I wrote . . .

Quick tears spring up again as I dress the dining room table for fall. The beautiful cocoa-colored tablecloth was a wedding present. I try to remember. How long ago was our wedding day? Thirty, thirty-four years? We would have been married thirty-four years. I'm getting older all the time. Will I be alone the rest of my life? Oh, Roger, how can I face another Thanksgiving without you? How can I watch as the summer sun fades softly into autumn, your favorite time of year?

He wrote . . .

"Even to your old age and gray hairs
I am he, I am he who will sustain
you.
I have made you and I will carry you;
I will sustain you and I will rescue
you."

Isaiah 46:4

I wrote . . .

I am drinking the bitter brew of pain, fear, lost love, loneliness, abandonment, frustration, the unknown. All is turbulence and confusion.

He wrote . . .

My soul finds rest in God alone;
  my salvation comes from him.
He alone is my rock and my salvation;
  he is my fortress, I will never be
    shaken.

Psalm 62:1–2

I wrote . . .

As I drove, I sobbed all the way home. How many times has this happened? Sometimes I can't even see to drive. I often think, "God must be steering for me right now." It's a wonder I haven't had any accidents.

He wrote . . .

The Lord will keep you from all harm—
he will watch over your life;
the Lord will watch over your coming
and going
both now and forevermore.

Psalm 121:7–8

I wrote . . .

My medication has not been 100 percent helpful. I'm using a new "prescription" out of desperation the last couple of mornings. This is the one that works! I pray Psalm 34 with my name in it. Boy is that powerful! I really tried this as a desperate, last-ditch attempt to overcome physical aches, fatigue, and depression. It's my morning "dose" for a while.

He wrote . . .

Phylis sought the Lord, and he answered
Phylis;
he delivered Phylis from all her fears.
Phylis looks to him and is radiant.
Her face is never covered with shame.
This poor *woman* called, and the Lord
heard Phylis;
he saved Phylis out of all her troubles.
The angel of the Lord encamps around
Phylis who fears him,
and he delivers Phylis.

Psalm 34:4–7, paraphrase

I wrote . . .

I go through storms of real physical need and temptation. These strong desires just cannot be fulfilled right now. Lord, I believe you can move heaven and earth and will provide a way of escape. I ask for that now.

He wrote . . .

None of the trials which have come upon you is more than a human being can stand. You can trust that God will not let you be put to the test beyond your strength, but with any trial will also provide a way out by enabling you to put up with it.

1 Corinthians 10:13 NJB

I wrote . . .

Fifth night of insomnia—you'd think I would be able to sleep. As I try to drift off, my heart starts doing wheelies—jolting, lurching, almost painful—just enough to jerk me awake. What is going on? Adrenaline? Not enough protein? (People heap me with their theories.) I know. It's "only" anxiety. Besides that, I've got these stupid, painful hangnails again—the straw that breaks the camel's back!

He wrote . . .

I have set the LORD always before me.
Because he is at my right hand,
I will not be shaken.
Therefore my heart is glad and my tongue
rejoices;
my body also will rest secure.

Psalm 16:8–9

I wrote . . .

Today is supposed to be our anniversary. It used to be my favorite day of the year. Now it only brings additional tears for an old wound that hasn't hurt this much for a long time. I try to forget about the date, but, truth is, I have a cramp in my heart.

He wrote . . .

"He will wipe every tear from their eyes. There will be no more death or mourning or crying or pain, for the old order of things has passed away."

Revelation 21:4

I wrote . . .

I now see bright possibilities of these verses becoming a reality for me!

He wrote . . .

I will exalt you, O Lord,
for you lifted me out of the depths
and did not let my enemies gloat over
me.
O Lord my God, I called to you for help
and you healed me.
O Lord, you brought me up from the
grave;
you spared me from going down into
the pit.
Sing to the Lord, you saints of his;
praise his holy name.
For his . . . favor lasts a lifetime;
weeping may remain for a night,
but rejoicing comes in the morning. . . .
You turned my wailing into dancing;
you removed my sackcloth and clothed
me with joy,
that my heart may sing to you and not be
silent.
O Lord my God, I will give you thanks
forever.

Psalm 30:1–5; 11–12

Acknowledgments

Second Corinthians 2:11 has been fulfilled as I trusted it would be—"On this we have set our hope that he will continue to deliver us, as you help us by your prayers. Then many will give thanks on our behalf for the gracious favor granted us in answer to the prayers of many." This book would not have become reality without the prayers of many. You who are one of the "many," thank you!

Thank you, Bonnie and Coleen, for believing, no, you even *knew* somehow, that God would see this done, even when I didn't believe it. Thank you, Sue Stewart, for suggesting that I record my thoughts, and then transcribing pages and pages from my journals. Thank you, Ruth Orlando, for seeing the invisible and writing to me years ago, assuring me that God would be faithful to bring me through the writing of this book. Thank you, David Kopp, for patient, good-humored support and advice over the last ten years.

Thanks to Lonnie Hull Dupont, my editor at Revell; Cheryl Van Andel; and Karen Steele, for quick responses to my questions and suggestions. You didn't leave me wondering. I am grateful.